LIFE ON MARS

Written by Tom Bradman

Illustrated by David Shephard

Hachette UK's policy is to use papers that are natural, renewable and recyclable products and made from wood grown in well-managed forests and other controlled sources. The logging and manufacturing processes are expected to conform to the environmental regulations of the country of origin.

ISBN: 9781398325401

Text © 2021 Tom Bradman
Illustrations, design and layout © Hodder & Stoughton Limited
First published in 2021 by Hodder & Stoughton Limited (for its Rising Stars imprint, part of the Hodder Education Group),
An Hachette UK Company
Carmelite House, 50 Victoria Embankment, London EC4Y 0DZ

www.risingstars-uk.com

Impression number 10 9 8 7 6 5 4 3 2
Year 2025 2024 2023 2022

Author: Tom Bradman
Series Editor: Tony Bradman
Commissioning Editor: Hamish Baxter
Illustrator: David Shephard/Bright International Group
Educational Reviewer: Helen Marron
Design concept and layouts: Lorraine Inglis Design
Editor: Amy Tyrer

With thanks to the schools that took part in the development of *Reading Planet* KS2, including: Ancaster CE Primary School, Ancaster; Downsway Primary School, Reading; Ferry Lane Primary School, London; Foxborough Primary School, Slough; Griffin Park Primary School, Blackburn; St Barnabas CE First & Middle School, Pershore; Tranmoor Primary School, Doncaster; and Wilton CE Primary School, Wilton.

All rights reserved. Apart from any use permitted under UK copyright law, no part of this publication may be reproduced or transmitted in any form or by any means, electronic or mechanical, including photocopying and recording, or held within any information storage and retrieval system, without permission in writing from the publisher or under licence from the Copyright Licensing Agency Limited. Further details of such licences (for reprographic reproduction) may be obtained from the Copyright Licensing Agency Limited, https://www.cla.co.uk/

A catalogue record for this title is available from the British Library.

Printed in the United Kingdom.

Orders: Please contact Hachette UK Distribution, Hely Hutchinson Centre, Milton Road, Didcot, Oxfordshire, OX11 7HH.

Telephone: (44) 01235 400555. Email: primary@hachette.co.uk

CONTENTS

1. How It Began 4
2. At Home 6
3. Dust Devils 14
4. Alone 20
5. The Pipeline 30
6. The Winner 38

1 HOW IT BEGAN

People have dreamed of living on Mars for hundreds of years.

One day soon, a spaceship will leave Earth to travel through space. It's going to be risky, but it will happen.

People will walk on the red sands of the red planet. They'll be scientists, learning more about this new world. It'll be difficult because there's no air to breathe or water to drink. They'll have to bring everything with them.

Some of them will go home, back to Earth, and others will stay.

Some will be builders and inventors. They'll build homes and machines to make the air.

There will be farmers, working inside buildings, growing food that would die outside.

It won't be easy or safe, but a city will grow and families will live there.

This is the story of one of the first children born on Mars: Kai.

You might think life on Mars will be exciting. Not for Kai. It's too risky to play outside. And there are no puddles to splash in or snowballs to throw at friends.

Kai hates having to stay inside.

2 AT HOME

Green leaves moved slowly in the air. Under them, fish swam in water, in between the roots that were hanging down, all held in a glass tank.

"This is where the farmers grow all of your food," said Mr Green, Kai's teacher.

The plants were impressive but Kai wasn't looking at the farm set-up. He was looking at what was behind the fish tank.

There was a big window and he could see the dusty red surface of the planet.

The surface of Mars.

"The water feeds the plants and the fish keep it clean," Mr Green went on. "If everything and everyone works together, no one need ever go hungry."

Kai wanted a challenge. He wanted to be outside, exploring, not on another school trip to another boring place.

"Are you listening, Kai?" the teacher asked.

"Of course," he said quickly. "You were talking about food and things."

Mr Green smiled. "I'm glad that you'll be prepared for the test later."

Kai swallowed.

Back at school, the test didn't go well. That would mean a difficult dinner with Dad later.

It was all boring. There was an alien world outside and he wasn't allowed to see it.

"It's time to talk about this term's project," Mr Green said. "You need to find out about our city and talk about things like the farm or making air or water."

"Fantastic," mumbled Kai. That sounded like lots of homework.

"Then," the teacher kept going, "you'll give a talk about everything you learn to the class."

Kai hated talking in front of the other pupils, he got so nervous.

"Ms Wang, our director, is going to choose the winner. And there's a prize," Mr Green said. "The best talk will win you a trip to the new space station."

Finally! Something exciting! This changed everything.

He didn't know how, but Kai knew he was going to win.

"How was school?" Dad asked at mealtime that evening.

"Fine," Kai said, pushing beans around his plate.

"What did you do today?" asked Desta, Dad's girlfriend. She'd been around a lot lately and Kai wasn't happy. She talked about her boring job too much. Desta ran the water department.

"Nothing," he replied. He just hoped they didn't ask about the test …

"Mr Green emailed me earlier," Dad said.

"Um, I …" Kai spluttered, avoiding his dad's eyes. "It's not an important test."

"It isn't really about the test, Kai," Dad told him. "But it shows you're not learning."

"Well, there's a contest now, a trip to the space station," Kai started talking fast. "I'm going to study, and give a talk, and do the best, and win."

"Okay," said Dad. "What will your talk be about?"

"I don't know yet."

"How about water?" Desta asked. "I think I can help."

"Yeah, maybe," Kai mumbled.

"I'm flying over the pipeline tomorrow," she went on. "You can help me check things, then tell the class about it."

"Really?" he shouted. "Flying across Mars?"

That sounded incredible! If only he didn't have to do it with Desta ...

The next morning, before he knew it, Kai was in a safety suit in the Mars-copter, next to Desta.

Then they were in the air.

A blanket of red land lay under them, a blue sky over them. Kai looked back at the city.

He had never been so far from home.

"Cool," he whispered.

"This should only take a few hours," Desta told him, watching the controls. "We need more water. We're using robots to build a pipe from the North Pole."

"Uh-huh," answered Kai, not really listening.

He wanted to be down there, on the sand.

"The problem is," she continued, "the robots stop working. Dust gets inside them. It's easy to fix. Open them up and blow some air in. But there isn't anyone to do it."

"Interesting," Kai mumbled, not interested at all.

A light flashed on the controls. On the horizon, a tower of dust reached up into the air.

"Oh no," Desta said. "Not now …"

"What?" Kai asked, worried.

"Put your helmet on," she replied. "That tower of dust is called a dust devil – and it's coming this way."

3 DUST DEVILS

"Hold on!" Desta shouted.

The Mars-copter jumped about in the wind. Kai could feel his toast bobbing around inside him.

"What's happening?" he asked. He could see more dust devils blocking their way.

"It's going to be bumpy, but we'll be okay," Desta said.

Her hands moved over the controls. They flew forwards, into the middle of the dust devils, swinging around them.

"There's a shelter close by," she said. "But we have to go through the dust devils."

Fear and excitement mixed together inside Kai's chest. Outside the window, the dust twisted and turned, and everything was red and brown. There were tiny sparks in the air, jumping about.

The copter shook, and went up and down and from side to side. He couldn't see the ground, only the dust.

Then an alarm started ringing.

"Desta?" he asked. "What's that?"

"A little motor problem …" she muttered.

More alarms started and warning lights blinked.

Desta battled with the copter.

Then, suddenly, they were down. Safe.

"You saved us!" Kai told her. Desta laughed.

"Don't thank me yet," she replied. "We've got quite a long walk outside."

They stood outside the copter. A metal rope connected Kai's belt to Desta's suit. She spoke through the speaker in Kai's helmet.

"Just remember," she said, "I'm with you."

He couldn't see far through the thick dust. Everything was dark and moving in the wind.

"One foot in front of the other," she told him. "You'll be home with your dad in no time."

"Okay," Kai replied.

This was his first time out on the surface of Mars. His suit kept him warm but a cold panic grew deep in his bones.

Then the lights started. Hundreds of tiny sparks jumped and skipped around him.

"It's static," Desta said. "From the dust. It can't hurt you, don't worry."

Kai lifted his hands and watched the lights skitter over them. He wanted to catch them, to play with them.

That's when he saw the shelter. They'd made it.

It was good to have some hot food in front of him. After the walk, he was even happy to be inside again. The shelter was a boring metal box, but at least it was something made by humans.

He was fed up with Mars after the morning they'd had.

"Where did you learn to fly?" Kai asked, in between bites of his microwave meal.

"On Earth, but it's very different here on Mars," Desta replied. "I can teach you when you're older, if you want?"

"Really?" he said. "That would be so cool!"

Maybe Desta wasn't too bad.

She was tapping at a computer and finally Dad appeared on the screen.

"Kai, how are you?" he asked. "I heard about the storm! I've been so worried!"

"I'm fine, Dad," Kai replied. "Desta did some amazing flying through the dust – and there was static and everything."

"Sounds exciting," Dad said.

"I'll tell you about it later," Desta told him. "But is the lift home coming soon?"

"There's a truck on the way," Dad replied. "But you need to know ... there's a problem with the pipeline."

4 ALONE

Dad told them that the robots kept failing and the pipeline wasn't working. There was too much water – it had nowhere to go. Soon, the water was going to destroy all the machines.

If they didn't complete the pipeline fast, everybody on Mars would be finished.

"Ernie is coming out with a truck to take you to try and save the pipeline."

"I'll come for you later Kai," Dad said. "I'm just waiting for the second truck to be set up. You'll have to wait there alone. It's only for a few hours."

"I want to help," Kai said. "It's important."

"I'm sorry," Desta said. "It's too risky. We're going to be driving into a growing dust storm. This isn't a game. It's serious and it's unsafe."

"But I can help," Kai argued. "You said we need the water."

"No, Kai," said Dad. "You're not going and that's the end of it."

Kai was angry and he refused to speak to Desta. He sat at the table they'd used for lunch and tapped at a tablet.

"I'm sorry, Kai," she said. "You'll understand when you're older."

"Whatever," he mumbled.

He tried to ignore her when she put her safety suit back on, and he didn't move when the truck arrived.

"We can talk when this is all over, okay?" she told him. "And I'll still teach you to fly, if you want."

"Fine," he muttered, not meaning it.

"I have to go now," Desta said. "Just stay here and wait for your dad."

"You said the pipeline was important," Kai almost shouted. "I want to help."

"You can't, Kai," she replied. "You have to stay here."

Then Desta went out and Kai was alone in the shelter. Inside again. Bored again.

After the flight, he'd thought Desta was cool. Now he was just angry at her.

Well, he was going to go with her, whether she wanted him to or not.

Kai had never put a safety suit on by himself before. But he knew what to do. They studied it every term at school.

He sneaked outside. Desta was on the truck and didn't see him.

The sky was blue again and there was no dust in the air.

"This looks safe to me," Kai said to himself.

The back of the truck was open, with lots of tools and boxes. He jumped on, just before the truck drove away.

It was a fast and bumpy ride. All the equipment was tied down with rope, but Kai wasn't.

He held on, but was still thrown from side to side.

There was one big bump and then he was up in the air. He landed hard, in the sand.

He looked up to see the truck drive away and disappear behind a hill.

He was alone.

Not like when he'd been in the shelter. People had made that.

Here, there was only the red sand and blue sky.

On the horizon, something big and dirty grew out of the ground. It was the dust storm Desta had told him about. It looked enormous and it was getting bigger.

He felt smaller than he ever had.

A map appeared on the inside of his helmet.

It showed him part of the pipeline and a robot. They looked a long way away.

The robot could carry him to another shelter.

He just had to get there. One foot in front of the other.

The storm grew on the horizon.

He hiked up one hill, and then another. His legs hurt. Walking in the safety suit wasn't easy.

Finally, he could see the pipeline.

He ran to the robot that stood next to it. It wasn't moving and it was easy to see why. There was dust all over it.

It had stopped working and he was stuck there.

He was in the middle of nowhere and there was only so much air in his suit.

He had no way to call for help. No one knew where he was.

Then he remembered!

Desta had told him how to fix the robots. Just open them up and blow some air in.

There was a cover on the back of the robot and Kai pulled it off. Under the cover, it was full of dust!

He used one of the pipes on his suit to blow air into the robot. The dust flew away and he could feel the robot turning on.

Yes, I did it! Kai grinned.

On the back of the robot's head, a computer screen lit up. On it, Kai could read the words WAITING FOR COMMANDS.

He tapped on the screen and a keyboard appeared. TAKE ME TO SAFETY, he keyed in.

The robot shuddered, lurched and then started moving.

Kai yelled in victory.

5 THE PIPELINE

Kai fell asleep riding the robot across Mars.

He dreamed he was underwater and couldn't breathe.

When he woke up, two people were carrying him through the doorway of another building. He could hear Desta speaking out of the microphone in his helmet.

"I'm sorry I left you, Kai," she said.

The robot hadn't taken him home. It had taken him to Desta at the North Pole.

Desta's workmate, Ernie, helped her take Kai's suit off and they gave him some hot tea. Kai's head pounded.

"You nearly ran out of air," Desta told him. "You could have died! What were you thinking?"

"I wanted to help," Kai said. He knew he had been stupid.

"If anything had happened to you ..." Desta started. "The water is only important if there are people, Kai. You're more important than any pipeline."

"I'm sorry," he said.

"It's okay," she replied. "You're safe now."

"But the pipeline still isn't up to the job," said Ernie.

Ernie continued, "There's too much water. It's going to destroy the machines soon."

"We have to do something," Desta said. "If that happens the city is finished."

"What about the pipeline?" Kai asked.

"It's nearly complete," Desta told him. "But the robots are all broken. We need the robots to finish the work."

"Can't you fix the robots?" Kai said.

"There just isn't time," Ernie said.

"There has to be!" Desta shouted. "We need to find the time!"

Kai thought about all that water and what people did with it at home. That reminded him of the school trip ...

"Wait," Kai said. "It's just like the school trip. We need to work together, like making food in the farms, like the fish and the plants."

"Even if the three of us started fixing the robots," Ernie answered, shaking his head, "we'd need forever. There are hundreds!"

"Not us," Kai told him. "Why don't we make the robots work together? They can fix each other."

Ernie hurried outside to fix the first robot.

Desta tapped in code quickly to teach the robots how to clean the dust out of each other.

Each one they fixed could then mend other robots. Soon they'd have hundreds, all set up to work.

For a while, things looked good. Robots went to work on the pipeline.

"It's too late," Ernie said, watching the work on a screen. "There's too much water. Any moment now, it's going to explode through."

"I'm going out there," Desta said. "The truck can push mud into the way and stop the water escaping."

"It's too risky," Ernie told her.

"There's no other way," she replied.

"I'll go with you," Kai said. He didn't want her to go, but he knew how difficult she was to stop.

"Not this time," Desta said, smiling at him. "You can help from here. We need you to check that the robots are doing their job."

Then she was gone.

Ernie showed Kai what to do and gave him control of a group of robots. All the robots were working again now, but they had so little time to finish the pipeline.

They worked fast and things came together, but more and more water kept coming.

Outside, Desta used the truck to push hills of mud around, stopping the water from escaping.

The robots moved more massive pipes into place and fixed them together.

Kai's hands moved over the controls, sending more robots to where they were needed. But they were running out of time ...

Then there was only one more piece of pipe to add.

All of a sudden water shot out of a hole. It flew up into the air, getting stronger and stronger. Driving the truck, Desta tried to cover the hole with more mud.

One of Kai's robots had the last bit of pipe. Kai focused. He sent the robot forwards and it jammed the piece of pipe in.

Ernie tapped a control and suddenly the water gushed into the pipe. "We did it!" they all yelled, jumping around and hugging each other.

6 THE WINNER

A few days later, Kai was back at the farm. He was watching the fish swimming underneath the plants. They were swimming in water from the pipeline, and that made him feel proud.

He'd given his talk to the class the day before, and everyone had been impressed.

Dad had even come to listen to him.

Desta appeared at the farm.

"Hi, Kai," she said. "Your dad told me the talk went well."

"It was okay," he replied.

"Just okay?" she asked. "So you didn't win? No flight to the space station?"

"Oh, I won," he told her with a huge grin. "And I can take a friend. Do you want to come?"

"Try to stop me!" she shouted. "But promise there aren't going to be any dust devils this time."

"Don't be silly," he laughed. "There are no dust devils where we're going. Now, solar storms on the other hand …"

CHAT ABOUT THE BOOK

1 Go to page 16. It was Kai's first time out on the surface of Mars. Why couldn't he see the land?

2 Read page 11. Why did Kai begin to talk fast?

3 When Kai gave his talk to the class everyone was impressed. What does 'impressed' mean?

4 How is the beginning of Kai's story and the end of the book linked?

5 Why do you think the author chose Mars as the setting for the story?

6 What would you like or dislike if you had to live on Mars like Kai?